Spot and Discover

DINOSAUR WORLD

William Potter

CONTENTS

Published in 2018 by **Windmill Books**, an Imprint of Rosen Publishing
29 East 21st Street, New York, NY 10010

Copyright © 2018 Windmill Books

Edited by Susannah Bailey | Written by William Potter | Illustrated by Matthew Scott | Designed by Trudi Webb and Emma Randall

CATALOGING-IN-PUBLICATION DATA
Names: Potter, William.
Title: Dinosaur world / William Potter.
Description: New York : Windmill Books, 2018. | Series: Spot and discover | Includes index.
Identifiers: LCCN ISBN 9781508193470 (pbk.) | ISBN 9781508193432 (library bound) |
ISBN 9781508193517 (6 pack)
Subjects: LCSH: Dinosaurs--Juvenile literature.
Classification: LCC QE861.5 P68 2018 | DDC 567.91--dc23

Manufactured in the United States of America
CPSIA Compliance Information: Batch BW18WM: For Further Information contact Rosen Publishing, New York, New York at 1-800-237-9932

Centrosaurus
(sen-tro-sore-us)
Centrosaurus was a horned, plant-eating
dinosaur that lived in a large herd.

Find 5

Pachyrhinosaurus
(pak-ee-rye-no-sore-us)
This elephant-sized dinosaur had
a horned plate protecting its head.

STAMPEDE!

**It's 75 million years ago and
a hungry Albertosaurus is on
the hunt. Run for your life!**

Find 4

Corythosaurus
(ko-rith-uh-sore-us)
These dinos called to each other
with loud, trumpetlike noises.

Find 8

Find 6

Atrociraptor
(a-TRO-see-rap-tor)
This small raptor would be only
a snack for Albertosaurus!

Find 5

Prosaurolophus
(pro-sore-rol-uh-fus)
The plant-eating Prosaurolophus
had a mouth like a duck's bill.

2

Find 5

Edmontonia
(ed-mon-toe-nee-uh)
This plant eater was built like a tank,
with spikes all over its back.

Find 7

Pachycephalosaurus
(pak-ee-sef-ul-lo-sore-us)
Pachycephalosaurus had a domed, spiky
skull it could use for head-butting.

Find 5

Lambeosaurus
(LAM-be-uh-sore-us)
A giant plant eater, Lambeosaurus
had two head crests and pebbly skin.

Euoplocephalus
(you-op-luh-SEF-uh-lus)
These dinos had hammer-like,
clubbed tails they could swing.

Find 3

Find 1

Albertosaurus
(al-bert-oh-sore-us)
This fast predator hunted
eight million years before T. rex.

Brachiosaurus
(BRACK-ee-uh-sore us)
This dino was so large, an adult human could only reach its knee.

Find 3

Hesperosaurus
(hes-pare-uh-sore-us)
A plant eater with round plates on its back, Hesperosaurus used its tail to defend itself.

Find 3

GRAZING GIANTS
The late Jurassic period was a time of giant, long-necked sauropods that ate from the tallest trees.

Apatosaurus
(ah-PAT-uh-sore-us)
Like all sauropods, Apatosaurus ate plants, such as conifers and ferns.

Find 3

Find 3

Find 5

Dryosaurus
(DRY-o-sore-us)
This ostrich-sized dino lived on leaves. Its name means "tree lizard."

Find 3

Allosaurus
(al-oh-sore-us)
Allosaurus was the biggest meat eater in North America.

4

Find 3

**Camarasaurus
(kuh-mare-uh-sore-us)**
A sauropod with a shorter neck
than others, it ate plants near the ground.

Find 3

**Gargoyleosaurus
(gar-goyl-ee-oh-sore-us)**
This dinosaur's spiky back
protected it from attack.

Find 3

**Stegosaurus
(STEG-uh-SORE-us)**
Stegosaurus had diamond-shaped
plates along its back and a spiked tail.

**Camptosaurus
(camp-tuh-sore-us)**
This plant-eating dinosaur
walked on two legs.

Find 3

**Diplodocus
(di-plo-do-kus)**
Although Dippy was one of the longest land
animals, it had one of the smallest brains.

Find 4

Thescelosaurus
(THES-kel-oh-sore-us)
This plant-eating dinosaur
was about as tall as a cow.

Champsosaurus
(CHAMP-soh-sore-us)
Champsosaurus was a reptile that
caught fish in its long, narrow jaws.

Find 13

SWAMP DWELLERS

Welcome to the swamp! Many different kinds of dinosaurs hunted and grazed here, alongside other prehistoric creatures.

Albertosaurus
(al-bert-oh-sore-us)
Albertosaurus, a fierce predator, could
run very fast on its strong back legs.

Find 4

Find 5

Adocus
(ah-DOH-kus)
This ancient reptile looked a
lot like today's turtles.

Find 3

Puertasaurus
(PWUHR-tah-sore-us)
Puertasaurus was as long as
three double-decker buses!

Find 4

**Triceratops
(try-SEH-rah-tops)**
Triceratops used its huge horns
to fight off fierce predators!

Find 8

**Pteranodon
(tuh-RAN-oh-don)**
Pteranodon, a flying reptile,
had a crest on its head.

Find 5

**Edmontosaurus
(ED-mon-toe-sore-us)**
This duck-billed dinosaur lived in
large groups and ate plants.

**Anzu
(AN-zoo)**
Anzu was a birdlike dinosaur, with
feathers, claws, and a beak!

Find 7

Find 3

**Ankylosaurus
(AN-kih-loh-sore-us)**
A plant-eating dinosaur that
had a club at the end of its tail.

7

Hylaeosaurus
(high-lee-oh-sore-us)
Hylaeosaurus, a plant eater, was one
of the first dinosaurs to be discovered.

Find 4

Eotyrannus
(ee-oh-ti-RAN-us)
Eotyrannus, a small raptor, was
an early relative of T. rex.

Find 3

Pelorosaurus
(pel-oh-ROW-sore-us)
This long-necked sauropod ate tough
plants with its super-strong teeth.

Find 3

FLOODLAND FEAST
125 million years ago, the sea levels rose and forests around the coasts became flooded.

Find 3

Baryonyx
(bare-ee-ON-ix)
These dinos might have used
their long claws to spear fish.

Find 7

Hypsilophodon
(hip-sih-lo-fuh-don)
Hypsilophodon, a fast plant eater,
was the size of a large dog.

8

Find 3

Becklespinax
(beck-el-spien-ax)
This meat-eating dinosaur would
have hunted Pelorosaurus.

Find 5

Iguanodon
(ig-wan-oh-don)
The fern-eating Iguanodon was one of the
first dinosaurs to be given a name.

Find 5

Neovenator
(nee-oh-ve-NAY-tor)
A small and fast raptor, it was
a threat to Iguanodon.

Valdosaurus
(VAL-doe-sore-us)
The name of this small
dinosaur means "forest lizard."

Find 4

Polacanthus
(pol-a-kan-thus)
This plant-eating dinosaur
had rows of spikes along its back.

Find 8

**Troodon young
(TRO-uh-don)**
Hatchlings had tiny feathers,
just like their parents.

Find 9

Find 2

**Troodon
(TRO-uh-don)**
Troodon was a goose-like dinosaur that sat
on and guarded a nest of up to 24 eggs.

BABY BITERS
Baby dinosaurs were born from eggs.
The parents sometimes protected
their nests from hungry visitors.

**Parasaurolophus
(par-ah-sore-OL-uh-fus)**
The crest on this dino's head
was a long, hollow tube.

Find 4

Find 5

Dragonflies
Prehistoric dragonflies were much
bigger than today's insects.

Find 3

**Edmontosaurus
(ed-mon-tuh-sore-us)**
This plant-eating dinosaur had about
1,000 diamond-shaped teeth.

Find 3

Panoplosaurus
(pan-OP-luh-sore-us)
Panoplosaurus was protected by a
tough back and spikes on its shoulders.

Find 6

Brachychamsa
(brack-ee-CHAM-sa)
This early alligator lurked in the
water, eyeing the hatchlings hungrily.

Find 6

Hadrosaurus
(HAD-ruh-sore-us)
Hadrosaurus dug hollows in
the ground to make nests.

Helopanoplia
(hel-o-pan-OP-li-a)
This early turtle lived
mostly in the water.

Find 3

Triceratops
(try-sair-uh-tops)
A bulky dinosaur that weighed the
same as two African elephants.

Find 4

11

Pterodactylus
(ter-oh-DAK-til-us)
Pterodactylus had wings made of skin stretched between its arms and legs.

Gnathosaurus
(NATH-oh-sore-us)
This pterosaur had a spoon-shaped beak and teeth as sharp as needles.

FLYING HIGH

150 million years ago, large reptiles called pterosaurs ruled the skies, along with the first birds.

Anurognathus
(an-YOOR-og-NATH-us)
Anurognathus, a small, flying creature, fed on insects such as damselflies.

Dakosaurus
(dack-oh-sore-us)
Dakosaurus, a huge, toothy sea monster, was related to the crocodile.

Aerodactylus
(air-oh-dak-til-us)
This duck-sized pterosaur was named after a Pokémon character.

**Scaphognathus
(sca-fog-nayth-us)**
Scaphognathus had a long tail
and a bony crest on its head.

**Rhamphorhynchus
(ram-for-ink-us)**
This pterosaur scooped up fish
with its curved beak full of teeth.

Find 8

**Dimorphodon
(di-MORF-oh-don)**
Dimorphodon was a large-headed pterosaur
that hunted small prey, including insects.

**Archaeopteryx
(ar-kee-OP-ter-ix)**
This early bird was the size of a
pigeon, and had claws on its wings.

Find 4

Find 9

**Libellulium
(li-bel-lul-ee-um)**
The prehistoric dragonfly, Libellulium,
was as big as a sparrow.

Xiphactinus
(zee-fact-in-us)
Xiphactinus, a large, fanged fish, was a strong swimmer that hunted smaller fish.

Find 5

Hybodus
(HY-bo-dus)
A prehistoric fish that looked like a great white shark, but was much smaller.

Find 4

SAVAGE SEAS
The prehistoric oceans were home to large reptiles who were just as dangerous as the dinosaurs on land.

Ichthyosaur
(ICK-thi-o-sore)
This predator looked like a dolphin with large eyes and a jaw full of sharp teeth.

Find 8

Find 3

Elasmosaurus
(ee-LAZ-mo-sore-us)
A fish-hunting reptile, it had a neck as long as its body!

Find 5

Kronosaurus
(crow-no-sore-us)
Kronosaurus was the size of a small whale and a dangerous predator.

14

Find 7

Archelon
(ar-kel-on)
Archelon was one of the largest
turtles to have ever lived.

Find 9

Protosphyraena
(pro-toss-fy-ray-na)
This swordfish-like creature had lots
of razor-sharp teeth.

Find 3

Mosasaurus
(MOSS-a-sore-us)
The largest of the underwater predators,
this lizard was the "T. rex of the seas."

Ammonite
(AM-on-ite)
This squid-like creature grew from thumb
size to the size of a tractor wheel.

Find 5

Nautilus
(naw-til-us)
Nautilus, a shelled, tentacled creature,
is still found in today's oceans.

Find 10

15

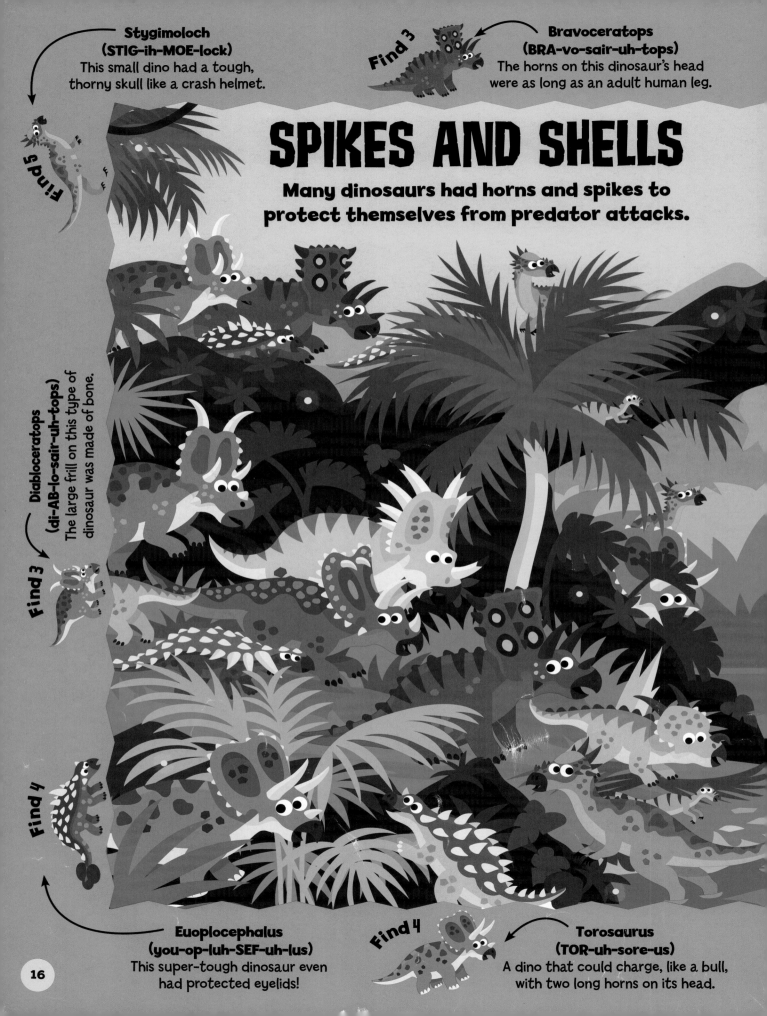

Stygimoloch
(STIG-ih-MOE-lock)
This small dino had a tough,
thorny skull like a crash helmet.

Find 3

Bravoceratops
(BRA-vo-sair-uh-tops)
The horns on this dinosaur's head
were as long as an adult human leg.

Find 5

SPIKES AND SHELLS

Many dinosaurs had horns and spikes to protect themselves from predator attacks.

Find 3

Diabloceratops
(di-AB-lo-sair-uh-tops)
The large frill on this type of
dinosaur was made of bone.

Find 4

Euoplocephalus
(you-op-luh-SEF-uh-lus)
This super-tough dinosaur even
had protected eyelids!

Find 4

Torosaurus
(TOR-uh-sore-us)
A dino that could charge, like a bull,
with two long horns on its head.

Find 3

Styracosaurus
(stih-RAK-uh-sore-us)
The horned frill around this dino's head looked like a crown.

Find 3

Ankylosaurus
(AN-kih-loh-sore-us)
Ankylosaurus, a bus-sized dinosaur, had a clubbed tail to swing at attackers.

Find 2

Pentaceratops
(PEN-tah-sair-uh-tops)
Pentaceratops had the largest skull ever found for a land animal.

Edmontonia
(ed-mon-toe-nee-uh)
This plant eater kept predators away with its thorny spikes.

Find 4

Find 4

Einiosaurus
(EYE-nee-o-sore-us)
An odd-looking dino with a horn on its nose that pointed down.

17

LAST DAYS

65 millions years ago, the dinosaurs began to die out after a large asteroid hit Earth, causing the sky to darken.

Gastonia
(gas-TOE-nee-uh)
The spikes on this dinosaur's tail could be used as a weapon.

Find 6

Deinonychus
(dye-NON-ik-us)
Deinonychus, a fast and feathered raptor, had long and very sharp claws.

Find 3

Quetzalcoatlus
(ket-sull-ko-at-lus)
The largest flying animal of all time. Quetzalcoatlus was the size of a small plane!

Find 3

Find 4

Achelousaurus
(ah-KEL-oo-sore-us)
This dino had a parrot-like beak and a protective bone frill over its neck.

Find 3

Tenontosaurus
(teh-NON-tuh-sore-us)
Tenontosaurus had a long, heavy tail that it used for balance.

Find 3

Bravoceratops
(BRA-vo-sair-uh-tops)
Without sunlight plants died, and plant eaters,
like these Bravoceratops, could not find food.

Find 2

Alamosaurus
(AL-uh-mo-sore-us)
Many of the trees this dino would
have fed on were burnt in wildfires.

Find 8

Orodromeus
(OR-uh-DROM-ee-us)
Orodromeus, a small plant eater,
may have dug burrows.

Protohadros
(proh-toh-HAD-ros)
"Duck-billed" dinosaurs, like this,
were called hadrosaurs.

Find 3

Find 4

Gryposaurus
(GRYE-puh-sore-us)
This dinosaur had skin covered in smooth
scales the size of fingernails.

Find 3

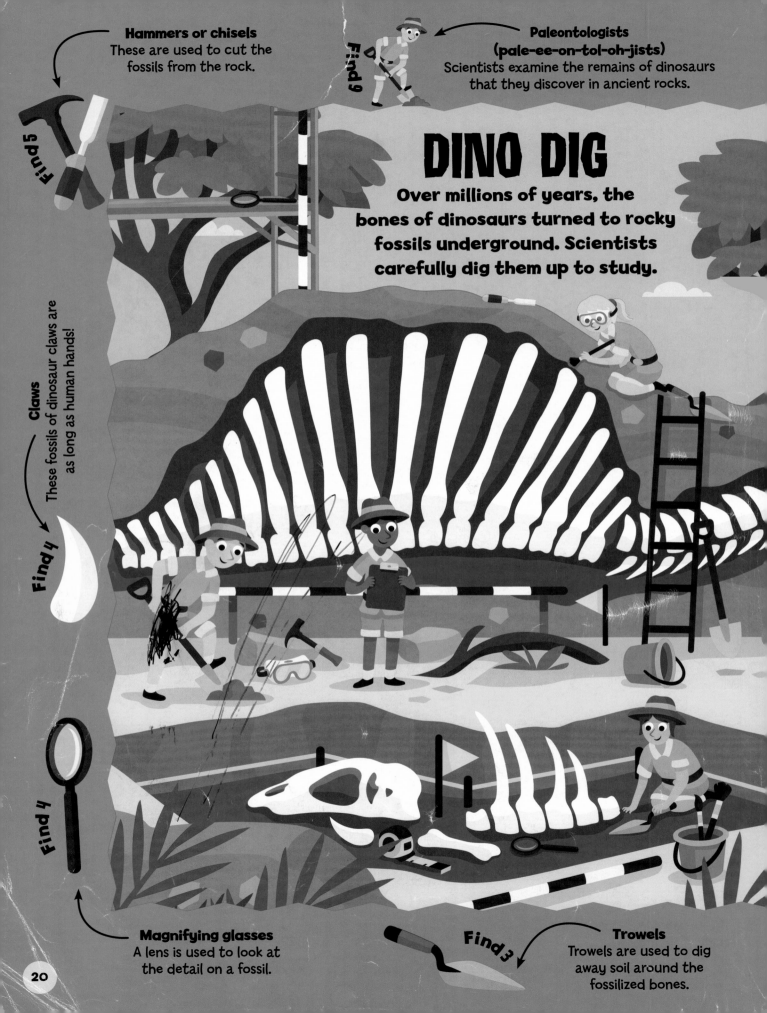

Hammers or chisels
These are used to cut the fossils from the rock.

Find 5

Paleontologists
(pale-ee-on-tol-oh-jists)
Scientists examine the remains of dinosaurs that they discover in ancient rocks.

Find 9

DINO DIG

Over millions of years, the bones of dinosaurs turned to rocky fossils underground. Scientists carefully dig them up to study.

Claws
These fossils of dinosaur claws are as long as human hands!

Find 4

Find 4

Magnifying glasses
A lens is used to look at the detail on a fossil.

Find 3

Trowels
Trowels are used to dig away soil around the fossilized bones.

Find 6

Brushes
Brushes are used to gently clean dust and soil from a fossil.

Find 3

Find 4

Buckets
Before a fossil is moved, it is covered in cloth and plaster for protection.

Safety goggles
When hammering rock, goggles protect the scientists' eyes from stone splinters.

Find 5

Thigh bones
These large dinosaur leg bones have been turned into rock over millions of years.

Find 3

21

Answers

2-3 STAMPEDE!

- Pachyrhinosaurus
- Centrosaurus
- Corythosaurus
- Atrociraptor
- Prosaurolophus
- Albertosaurus
- Euoplocephalus
- Lambeosaurus
- Pachycephalosaurus
- Edmontonia

4-5 GRAZING GIANTS

- Brachiosaurus
- Hesperosaurus
- Apatosaurus
- Dryosaurus
- Allosaurus
- Diplodocus
- Camptosaurus
- Stegosaurus
- Gargoyleosaurus
- Camarasaurus

6–7 SWAMP DWELLERS

- Champsosaurus
- Thescelosaurus
- Albertosaurus
- Adocus
- Puertasaurus
- Ankylosaurus
- Anzu
- Edmontosaurus
- Pteranodon
- Triceratops

8-9 FLOODLAND FEAST

- Eotyrannus
- Hylaeosaurus
- Pelorosaurus
- Baryonyx
- Hypsilophodon
- Polacanthus
- Valdosaurus
- Neovenator
- Iguanodon
- Becklespinax

10-11 BABY BITERS

- Troodon
- Troodon young
- Parasaurolophus
- Dragonflies
- Edmontosaurus
- Triceratops
- Helopanoplia
- Hadrosaurus
- Brachychamsa
- Panoplosaurus

Answers

12-13 FLYING HIGH

- Gnathosaurus
- Pterodactylus
- Anurognathus
- Dakosaurus
- Aerodactylus
- Libellulium
- Archaeopteryx
- Dimorphodon
- Rhamphorhynchus
- Scaphognathus

14-15 SAVAGE SEAS

- Hybodus
- Xiphactinus
- Ichthyosaur
- Elasmosaurus
- Kronosaurus
- Nautilus
- Ammonite
- Mosasaurus
- Protosphyraena
- Archelon

16-17 SPIKES AND SHELLS

- Bravoceratops
- Stygimoloch
- Diabloceratops
- Euoplocephalus
- Torosaurus
- Einiosaurus
- Edmontonia
- Pentaceratops
- Ankylosaurus
- Styracosaurus

18-19 LAST DAYS

- Deinonychus
- Gastonia
- Quetzalcoatlus
- Achelousaurus
- Tenontosaurus
- Gryposaurus
- Protohadros
- Orodromeus
- Alamosaurus
- Bravoceratops

20-21 DINO DIG

- Palaeontologists
- Hammers or chisels
- Claws
- Magnifying glasses
- Trowels
- Thigh bones
- Safety goggles
- Buckets
- Tape measures
- Brushes

Glossary

asteroid A rocky body that orbits the Sun in space.

crest A prominent sail-like feature that stands up from the head or neck of some animals.

Cretaceous A period of time, around 145 million years ago, following the Jurassic period.

Jurassic A period of time, around 200 million years ago, followed by the Cretaceous period.

predator A creature that hunts other creatures for food.

raptor A type of dinosaur that stands on two legs and has sharp claws.

reptile A cold-blooded creature, with skin covered in scales.

sauropod A plant-eating dinosaur with a heavy body, long neck and tail, which lived on land.

Further Information

BOOKS

Atlas of Dinosaur Adventures: Step Into a Prehistoric World by Emily Hawkins, Wide Eyed Editions, 2017.

Dinosaurs (Collins Fascinating Facts), Collins, 2016.

Dinosaur Atlas (Slide and Discover) by Dr. Jen Green, Silver Dolphin Books, 2014.

The Birth of the Dinosaurs (Planet Earth) by Michael Bright, Wayland Books, 2017.

WEBSITES

For web resources related to the subject of this book, go to: **www.windmillbooks.com/weblinks** and select this book's title.

Index